The Civil War in the West

Untold History of the Civil War

CHELSEA HOUSE PUBLISHERS

Untold History of the Civil War

The Civil War in the West

Douglas J. Savage

CHELSEA HOUSE PUBLISHERS
Philadelphia

Produced by Combined Publishing
P.O. Box 307, Conshohocken, Pennsylvania 19428
1-800-418-6065
E-mail:combined@combinedpublishing.com
web:www.combinedpublishing.com

CHELSEA HOUSE PUBLISHERS

Editor in Chief: Stephen Reginald
Managing Editor: James D. Gallagher
Production Manager: Pamela Loos
Art Director: Sara Davis
Director of Photography: Judy L. Hasday
Senior Production Editor: LeeAnne Gelletly
Assistant Editor: Anne Hill

Front Cover Illustration: "The Color Guard of Texas" by Keith Rocco. Courtesy of
Tradition Studios ©Keith Rocco.

35798642

Library of Congress Cataloging-in-Publication Data applied for:
ISBN 0-7910-5437-3

Contents

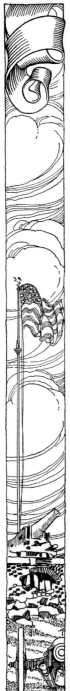

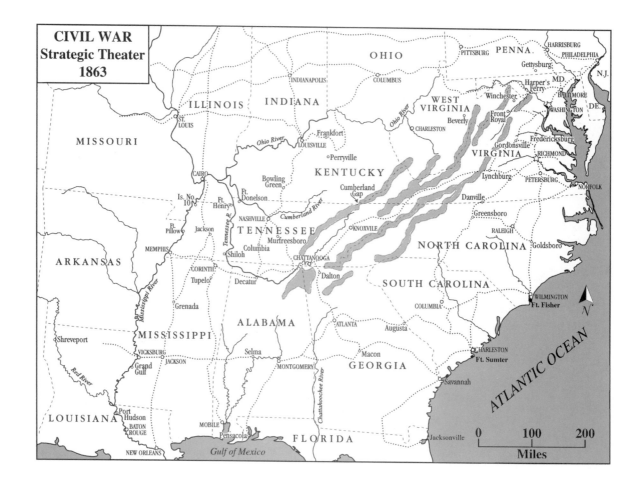

CIVIL WAR
Strategic Theater
1863

OHIO

PITTSBURG   PENNA.   HARRISBURG
PHILADELPHIA

Gettysburg
INDIANAPOLIS   COLUMBUS   WEST   Winchester   Harper's   MD.   N.J.
VIRGINIA   Ferry   BALTIMORE

ILLINOIS   INDIANA   Beverly   Front   WASHINGTON   DE.
Royal
ST.   CHARLESTON   Gordonsville   Fredericksburg
LOUIS   Ohio River

MISSOURI   Frankfort   VIRGINIA   RICHMOND
Ohio River   LOUISVILLE
Perryville   Lynchburg   PETERSBURG   NORFOLK

CAIRO   KENTUCKY   Danville
Bowling   Cumberland
Green   Gap   Greensboro
Is. No.   Ft.   Ft.   Cumberland River   RALEIGH
10   Henry   Donelson   KNOXVILE   Goldsboro
FT.   NASHVILLE   NORTH CAROLINA
Pillow   Jackson   TENNESSEE   Murfreesboro
MEMPHIS   Columbia   CHATTANOOGA   SOUTH CAROLINA   WILMINGTON
Shiloh   Dalton   Ft. Fisher
ARKANSAS   CORINTH   Decatur
Tupelo   COLUMBIA

Grenada   ATLANTA   Augusta   CHARLESTON
ALABAMA   Ft. Sumter   ATLANTIC OCEAN
Shreveport   Macon
MISSISSIPPI   Selma   GEORGIA
VICKSBURG   Savannah
Grand   JACKSON   MONTGOMERY
Gulf   Red River

LOUISIANA   Port
Hudson   MOBILE   Jacksonville   0   100   200
BATON   Pensacola   FLORIDA
ROUGE   Gulf of Mexico   Miles
NEW ORLEANS

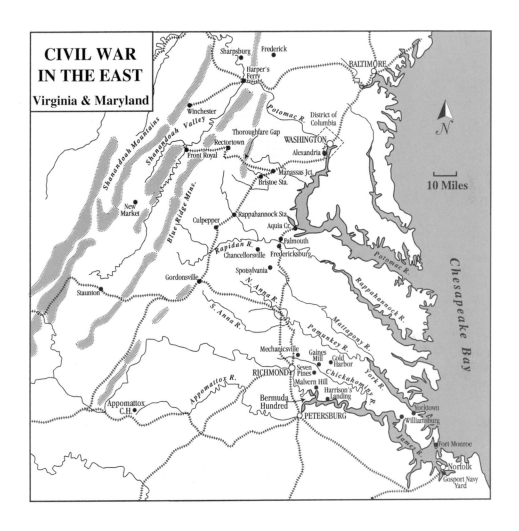

**CIVIL WAR
IN THE EAST**

Virginia & Maryland

N

10 Miles

Sharpsburg

Frederick

Harper's
Ferry

BALTIMORE

Winchester

Potomac R.

District of
Columbia

Shanandoah Mountains

Shanandoah Valley

Thoroughfare Gap

Rectortown

WASHINGTON

Front Royal

Alexandria

Manassas Jct.

Bristoe Sta.

New
Market

Blue Ridge Mtns.

Rapidan R.

Rappahannock Sta.

Culpepper

Aquia Cr.

Falmouth

Potomac R.

Chancellorsville

Fredericksburg

Spotsylvania

Rappahannock R.

Gordonsville

N. Anna R.

Staunton

S. Anna R.

Chesapeake Bay

Mattapony R.

Pamunkey R.

Mechanicsville

Gaines
Mill

Cold
Harbor

Seven
Pines

RICHMOND

Chickahominy R.

Malvern Hill

York R.

Appomattox R.

Harrison's
Landing

Bermuda
Hundred

Yorktown

Appomattox
C.H.

PETERSBURG

Williamsburg

James R.

Fort Monroe

Norfolk

Gosport Navy
Yard

Civil War Chronology

1860

November 6 Abraham Lincoln is elected president of the United States.

December 20 South Carolina becomes the first state to secede from the Union.

1861

January-April Mississippi, Florida, Alabama, Georgia, Louisiana, and Texas also secede from the Union.

April 1 Bombardment of Fort Sumter begins the Civil War.

April-May Lincoln calls for volunteers to fight the Southern rebellion, causing a second wave of secession with Virginia, Arkansas, Tennessee, and North Carolina all leaving the Union.

May Union naval forces begin blockading the Confederate coast and reoccupying some Southern ports and offshore islands.

July 21 Union forces are defeated at the battle of First Bull Run and withdraw to Washington.

1862

February Previously unknown Union general Ulysses S. Grant captures Confederate garrisons in Tennessee at Fort Henry (February 6) and Fort Donelson (February 16).

March 7-8 Confederates and their Cherokee allies are defeated at Pea Ridge, Arkansas.

March 8-9 Naval battle at Hampton Roads, Virginia, involving the USS *Monitor* and the CSS *Virginia* (formerly the USS *Merrimac*) begins the era of the armored fighting ship.

April-July The Union army marches on Richmond after an amphibious landing. Confederate forces block Northern advance in a series of battles. Robert E. Lee is placed in command of the main Confederate army in Virginia.

April 6-7 Grant defeats the Southern army at Shiloh Church, Tennessee, after a costly two-day battle.

April 27 New Orleans is captured by Union naval forces under Admiral David Farragut.

May 31 The battle of Seven Pines (also called Fair Oaks) is fought and the Union lines are held.

August 29-30 Lee wins substantial victory over the Army of the Potomac at the battle of Second Bull Run near Manassas, Virginia.

September 17 Union General George B. McClellan repulses Lee's first invasion of the North at Antietam Creek near Sharpsburg, Maryland, in the bloodiest single day of the war.

November 13 Grant begins operations against the key Confederate fortress at Vicksburg, Mississippi.

December 13 Union forces suffer heavy losses storming Confederate positions at Fredericksburg, Virginia.

1863

January 1 President Lincoln issues the Emancipation Proclamation, freeing the slaves in the Southern states.

May 1-6	Lee wins an impressive victory at Chancellorsville, but key Southern commander Thomas J. "Stonewall" Jackson dies of wounds, an irreplaceable loss for the Army of Northern Virginia.
June	The city of Vicksburg and the town of Port Hudson are held under siege by the Union army. They surrender on July 4.
July 1-3	Lee's second invasion of the North is decisively defeated at Gettysburg, Pennsylvania.
July 16	Union forces led by the black 54th Massachusetts Infantry attempt to regain control of Fort Sumter by attacking the Fort Wagner outpost.
September 19-20	Confederate victory at Chickamauga, Georgia, gives some hope to the South after disasters at Gettysburg and Vicksburg.

1864

February 17	A new Confederate submarine, the *Hunley*, attacks and sinks the USS *Housatonic* in the waters off Charleston.
March 9	General Grant is made supreme Union commander. He decides to campaign in the East with the Army of the Potomac while General William T. Sherman carries out a destructive march across the South from the Mississippi to the Atlantic coast.
May-June	In a series of costly battles (Wilderness, Spotsylvania, and Cold Harbor), Grant gradually encircles Lee's troops in the town of Petersburg, Richmond's railway link to the rest of the South.
June 19	The siege of Petersburg begins, lasting for nearly a year until the end of the war.
August 27	General Sherman captures Atlanta and begins the "March to the Sea," a campaign of destruction across Georgia and South Carolina.
November 8	Abraham Lincoln wins reelection, ending hope of the South getting a negotiated settlement.
November 30	Confederate forces are defeated at Franklin, Tennessee, losing five generals. Nashville is soon captured (December 15-16).

1865

April 2	Major Petersburg fortifications fall to the Union, making further resistance by Richmond impossible.
April 3-8	Lee withdraws his army from Richmond and attempts to reach Confederate forces still holding out in North Carolina. Union armies under Grant and Sheridan gradually encircle him.
April 9	Lee surrenders to Grant at Appomattox, Virginia, effectively ending the war.
April 14	Abraham Lincoln is assassinated by John Wilkes Booth, a Southern sympathizer.

Union Army
Army of the Potomac
Army of the James
Army of the Cumberland

Confederate Army
Army of Northern Virginia
Army of Tennessee

Captain Nathaniel Lyon fought at the head of the Union troops in Missouri.

I

"Put Your Soul in the Effort"

Most Civil War history concentrates on the battles and generals of the eastern theater. Virginia and Virginians dominate the histories and the collective memory of our country. This is true for two reasons: first, the eastern battles, such as Antietam, Fredericksburg, Gettysburg, the Wilderness, and the siege of Petersburg were huge and ferocious. Second, few historical figures can match the color, the glory, or the victories of Robert E. Lee, Stonewall Jackson, and Ulysses S. Grant.

But the terrible war which divided the country during four years of bloodshed was not won or lost in Virginia, nor at Gettysburg, Pennsylvania. As Professor James M. McPherson of Princeton University argued, "The Union ultimately won the war mainly by victories in the West."

Not only did the North win the Civil War by winning the West—the war really began there, too.

★ ★ ★

We think of the Civil War as beginning in April 1861 at Fort Sumter, South Carolina. That was indeed the first shot, but the American Civil War really began out West 40 years before Fort Sumter. The seeds of the war were planted in the Missouri Compromise of 1820.

Thomas Jefferson's Louisiana Purchase in 1803 doubled the size of the United States. But the slavery issue created a crisis in the new land. Would the vast wilderness purchased from France be open to slavery? Seventeen years later, Congress passed the Missouri Compromise, also known as the Compromise of 1820, to settle the question. The Compromise declared that slavery would never extend north of $36\frac{1}{2}$ degrees north latitude, with the exception of the new state of Missouri which would be admitted to the Union as a slave state. Twenty-seven years later, the Mexican War created a similar political problem.

When the Treaty of Guadalupe Hidalgo ended the 1846-1847 Mexican War, the United States acquired huge new lands west of the Louisiana Purchase area. The treaty brought in territories which would later become the states of Texas, Arizona, New Mexico, Nevada, Utah, California, and parts of Colorado, Oklahoma, and Wyoming. Most of this area was south of the $36\frac{1}{2}$-degree no-slavery line. Northern, antislavery states objected to so much new slave territory becoming part of the country. When Congressman David Wilmot from Pennsylvania introduced a bill outlawing slavery in any land won from Mexico, into the United States Congress in 1846, the Wilmot Proviso passed the House of Representatives but was defeated by the Senate.

After the Mexican War, another Congressional compromise had to resolve the issue of which new territories would allow slavery and which would be antislavery. Congress ducked the issue by passing the

Compromise of 1850. It admitted California into the Union as an antislavery, free state, but put off the question of slavery in the other new territories until each territory applied for statehood in the future—this put the final conflict off for only four years.

When Kansas and Nebraska applied for statehood, the slavery question had to be faced again. The Kansas-Nebraska Act of 1854 admitted Nebraska as a free state and Kansas as a slave state. The act also repealed the 36½-degree no-slavery line. Each new state would be allowed to decide for itself whether to enter the Union as a slave state or a free state. This eliminated the 35-year-long procedure of admitting new states two at a time, one slave and one free, to maintain the delicate balance in Congress of slave and free states. One result of the Kansas-Nebraska Act was the February 1854 creation of the Republican Party in Ripon, Wisconsin, which opposed slavery in the western territories. Two years later, the United States Supreme Court declared that black people held in slavery were not human beings but property, and that Congress did not have the power to prevent slavery from spreading across the western territories. The infamous *Dred Scott* decision removed from Congress the authority to put civil war off for another generation. Five years later, Southerners fired upon the United States outpost at Fort Sumter, South Carolina. Within four years, nearly one million men in both the North and the South would die to end what the Louisiana Purchase had started.

Ulysses S. Grant led the Union army to victory on the Mississippi River and its tributaries.

II

War on the Rivers

*T*he landscape of the country in 1861 dictated that civil war in the East would be different from civil war in the American West. It was all about rivers.

In the East, important rivers run east and west. When the Northern armies set out in 1861 to conquer the Confederate States of America, the Federal armies moving southward had to cross the rivers in their way. The east-west rivers were natural barriers to "invading" armies. But in the West, the principal rivers run north and south. These rivers were water highways for Federal forces to enter the Confederacy from above and from below. Professor Richard M. McMurry of North Carolina State University put it simply: "[T]he Virginia rivers favored the Southerners; the western waters helped the Yankees."

And the river highway cutting through the very heart of the Confederate States of America was the Mississippi River. If the South could hold the Mississippi, the Confederacy could maintain connections with the entire continent all the way to the Pacific Ocean. But if the Federal armies could control

the Mississippi, the Confederacy would be cut in half. Abraham Lincoln knew this and he also knew the river—he had worked on a riverboat on the Mississippi as a boy.

During the second and third years of the war, President Lincoln worked to capture the Mississippi River. Without that waterway he knew the Confederacy would be crippled and starved into submission. The president's man for the job was a gruff, cigar-chomping soldier named Ulysses S. Grant.

Grant had entered the Union army as a captain and made colonel by mid-1861. By January 1862, Grant was a brigadier general, ready to begin his 18-month campaign to win the Mississippi River for the Federals. He began on two Tennessee rivers which empty into the Ohio River on its way to the Mississippi at Cairo, Illinois. These rivers were the Cumberland and the Tennessee.

The Confederacy knew the strategic importance of these two rivers flowing through Tennessee, Kentucky, and the Confederate heartland. The rivers form two sides of a triangle pointing southward in northwest Tennessee: the Ohio River is the upper, hor-

Union gunboats sail up the Cumberland River to capture Fort Donelson.

16

izontal side flowing west; the Tennessee River flows north toward the Ohio as the western side of the triangle; and, the Cumberland River also flows northward, forming the right, eastern side of the triangle. The strip of land between these rivers is 12 miles wide. Confederates manned Fort Henry on the east bank of the Tennessee River (the west side of the strip of land) and manned Fort Donelson on the west bank

Commodore Andrew Hull Foote was commander of the Union fleet that helped win Fort Donelson and Fort Henry for the Union.

of the Cumberland River (the east side of the strip). If the Union army could capture both forts, it would open the way for an upriver invasion of both Kentucky (which had forces fighting on both sides of the war) and Tennessee. If the Confederates could hang onto both forts, they could use western Tennessee and Kentucky as bases for protecting the northern Mississippi River up to Cairo, Illinois.

Grant concentrated his men in blue at Paducah, Kentucky, in January 1862. On January 30, Grant headed south with 23 regiments of infantry, supported on the Tennessee River by four new ironclad gunboats. Each steampowered boat was 175 feet long, 50 feet wide, and was protected by $2\frac{1}{2}$-inch iron armor. Each gunboat carried 13 cannons.

The ships were manned by army men, but they were commanded on the river by Commodore Andrew Hull Foote, who, at age 56, had spent 40 years in the United States Navy. In addition to the four ironclads, he also commanded three unarmored gunboats, and nine troop ships bearing half of Grant's 15,000 soldiers. After dropping these troops off near Panther Creek which flows into the Tennessee River three miles north of Fort Henry, Commodore Foote steamed 100 miles back to Paducah to pick up the other half of Grant's army. Grant's 15,000 men were divided into 1st Division and 2nd Division.

Fort Henry was defended by General Lloyd Tilghman with only 3,400 Confederates. Born in Maryland, 46-year-old Tilghman had graduated from West Point in 1836, but left the military to become a construction engineer for 25 years. His troops at Fort Henry were poorly armed with old flintlock, smooth-bore muskets and shotguns, many of which were left over from the War of 1812. Even the Tennessee River worked against him: high water had flooded half of his 15 cannons which faced the river and Grant's two divisions of blueclad infantry.

At noon on February 6, 1862, Commodore Foote's gunboats steamed toward Fort Henry. From a mile away, 54 cannons shelled the fort. The gunboats closed to within 600 yards of the fort. Even with their waterlogged cannons, Confederate guns managed to hit Foote's flagship 32 times. But the shells bounced off the ships' iron sides. While the gunboats and Rebel guns pounded each other, General Tilghman's outgunned troops escaped the fort and marched eastward to the protection of Fort Donelson on the Cumberland River. General Tilghman's brave cannoneers hung on until the gray infantry were safely away. Then he surrendered the fort to General Grant. The Confederates had lost 10 men killed and 11 wounded. The Yankees lost 12 killed and 27 wounded—all Federal casualties were on the gunboats, especially those which were not covered with armor plates.

With Fort Henry secured, Grant planned to march east to capture Fort Donelson which protected the mouth of the Cumberland River. Fort Donelson was not Fort Henry, with its flooded guns and flintlocks. Seventeen thousand Confederate infantry with 12 large cannons and several small cannons defended Donelson and the Cumberland, under the command of General John Floyd, a 55-year-old lawyer and former governor of Virginia.

At daybreak on February 13, 1862, General Grant's two divisions attacked Fort Donelson. General John A. McClernand commanded Grant's 1st Division, and General Charles F. Smith commanded Grant's 2nd Division. When General Grant was a cadet at West Point, Smith was superintendent of cadets. Now, Grant gave orders to his former teacher. Fighting was fierce all day. The Rebels beat back the blue 1st Division three times. General Smith's 2nd Division was repulsed once. As night approached, the gunplay stopped for the day. During the night, the temperature dropped to 13 degrees. Snow and sleet pelted the dead and wounded and many were frozen solid by morning.

By dawn the next day, February 14, Federal reinforcements arrived increasing Grant's force to 27,500 men. Commodore Foote brought his four ironclad gunboats up the Cumberland and shelled Fort Donelson from one mile away. By 3:00 P.M., the gunboats were 200 yards from the fort. The ships did all

General John A. McClernand led troops under General Grant during the battle for Fort Donelson.

Confederate General Gideon Pillow tried to hold Fort Donelson for the South.

the fighting that afternoon and Foote's crews suffered 11 men killed and 43 wounded.

On the third day at Fort Donelson, Confederate General Gideon Pillow attacked McClernand's Yankees. General McClernand, an Illinois congressman, fought desperately for three hours. General Pillow finally pulled back near the Tennessee hamlet of Dover.

On the fourth day, February 16, Federal artillery from the river again pounded the fort. Cut off from outside help, Fort Donelson surrendered. Before giving up the fort, Generals Floyd and Pillow escaped with a detachment of Confederate cavalry. They left behind 12,000 men and General Simon Buckner, who surrendered to Brigadier General Grant. Before the war, Grant and Buckner had been friends and Buckner had graduated one year behind Grant at West Point.

The fall of Forts Henry and Donelson were vital western victories for the Federals. Opening the Tennessee and Cumberland Rivers to invasion meant that President Lincoln could fight the Confederacy on its western side as well as in the east. It would now be a two-front war and a fight to the death. Lincoln rewarded Brigadier General Grant by promoting him to major general.

On the day that General Buckner surrendered Fort Donelson, President Lincoln did not yet know of General Grant's important victory. On that February 16, 1862, Lincoln wrote a telegram to Major General Henry Halleck, who was General Grant's commanding officer in St. Louis, Missouri. President Lincoln wrote: "Our success or failure at Donelson is vastly important; and I beg you to put your soul in the effort."

General Halleck did not have to put his own soul into the fight—Grant did it for him.

Colonel Benjamin Grierson led the 6th Illinois Cavalry on a daring raid into Mississippi.

III

The Father of Waters

The opening of western Tennessee and Kentucky was important to the Union cause. But the Federal victories at Forts Henry and Donelson would mean nothing unless the vital Mississippi River could be opened to Yankee armies and navies. The key to the river was the city of Vicksburg, Mississippi. In Major General Grant, President Lincoln had found the man to turn that key.

The county in which Vicksburg sat had 11,000 people—nearly 10,000 of them were slaves. The homes of Vicksburg and Warren County were built by slaves, and the crops which the county ate or sold were tilled by slaves. "It may be argued," Dr. Peter Walker of the University of North Carolina wrote 100 years later, "that the city existed because of the slaves."

Mounted high above the Mississippi, Vicksburg's Confederate cannons controlled the middle of the river, halfway between Memphis, Tennessee, and Baton Rouge, Louisiana. If the Yankees could capture New Orleans, Louisiana, at the mouth of the river and Vicksburg, Mississippi, at its center, then Union gun-

boats and ironclads on the river would cut the Confederacy in half.

Federal hopes ran high on April 25, 1862, when New Orleans fell to the Yankees, opening the southern delta of the Mississippi to Northern forces. By the first of May, Confederate troops, mostly artillerymen, began marching into Vicksburg to fortify the city and to hold the upper Mississippi for the Confederacy. If Memphis, Tennessee, fell to the Yankees, Vicksburg would become the final Confederate fortress guarding the great river. Memphis would fall in June.

On May 12, 1862, Martin Luther Smith arrived at Vicksburg to command its defenses. General Smith supervised the placement of 18 cannons behind the city on the cliffs, 200 feet above the Mississippi. Six days later, a Sunday, a Yankee fleet steamed upriver from New Orleans. Five Yankee gunboats and two troop ships dropped anchor under the command of Captain S. Phillips Lee of the United States Navy. Lee sent messages ashore which demanded the surrender of the city. Two days later on May 18, Mayor Laz Lindsay replied for the 5,000 loyal Confederate citizens of Vicksburg: "[N]either the municipal authorities nor the citizens will ever consent to a surrender of the city." The brave civilians and their defenders in gray kept their word for the next 14 months.

On May 20, 1862, Captain Lee's gunboats began firing at Rebel infantry on the high cliffs—the first shots of the siege of Vicksburg. The next day, Captain Lee gave the city authorities 24 hours to evacuate civilians from the new battle zone and on May 22, a Yankee naval gun lobbed 11-inch shells, each weighing 166 pounds, toward the town.

But the high bluffs towering above the Mississippi blocked the naval bombardment. The gunboats were too low in the water to get their shells over the cliffs and into the city. So by June 2, the fleet added mortars to their artillery arsenal. The mortars could lob shells high up and over the bluffs, and down the backside of Vicksburg. Civilians who had not evacuated began digging little bombshelters in their yards so they could live underground when the shells arced overhead.

When Memphis, Tennessee, finally fell to the Federals on June 6, Vicksburg found itself trapped between Yankees upriver and Yankees downriver. The city on the cliffs could be shelled now from Federal gunboats sailing down from Memphis or sailing up from New Orleans. A Federal fleet sailed downriver from the north and the United States Navy's assault on Vicksburg from two directions began on June 26.

Next day, the Federal fleet shelled the city all day. That night at 3:00 in the morning, the Federals launched their first night bombardment of Vicksburg. Yankee shells exploded in the city for five hours. While the mortars fell, the Northern fleet steamed past the city's high cannons, joined the Southern fleet, and the shelling continued into June 30. To celebrate the Fourth of July 1862, the Federal fleet lobbed 150 shells into the town.

The one-sided naval contest changed for a moment on July 15. Three days earlier, the Confederate ironclad, CSS *Arkansas*, sailed south from the Yazoo River into the Mississippi toward Vicksburg. Her path was open since the Yankee fleet once north of town had joined the fleet south of Vicksburg. On the 15th, the *Arkansas* steamed directly into the Yankee ships. Running through a gauntlet of 37 Federal gunboats, she damaged three Federal warships. Then the *Arkansas* and her heroic crew slipped through the Yankee fleet and docked at Vicksburg. It was welcomed by cheering Confederates. On July 22, three

The Rebel ship Arkansas *tried to run the Union blockade at Vicksburg, Mississippi.*

Federal ships attacked the Rebel ironclad but were driven off. Shelling continued for two days.

The Rebels of Vicksburg had another weapon on the river—mosquitos. By the third week of July, malaria had ravaged the Yankee fleet. Two thousand four hundred sailors were sick. So on July 24, the Federal fleet shelled the city one last time and then most of the fleet sailed north to anchor 12 miles upriver on the Yazoo while part of the fleet fled south. Only two gunboats were left behind to patrol the city's stretch of river. The town was quiet for three months.

The fight for Vicksburg continued in the fall with military maneuvers. On October 14, 1862, Major General John C. Pemberton took command of the Confederacy's 22,000-man Department of Mississippi including Vicksburg. Though a Northerner by birth, General Pemberton's loyalties were Confederate. On October 16, 1862, General Ulysses Grant was given command of the North's Department of the Tennessee which included Vicksburg. Grant's army numbered 40,000.

In November, Grant's supply base was at Grand Junction in southwest Tennessee. He marched his army southward toward Vicksburg and established a supply depot at Holly Springs, Mississippi, 200 miles north of Vicksburg. As Grant pressed slowly south, he left Holly Springs behind him, guarded only by 1,500 men. On December 20, Confederate General Earl Van Dorn led 3,500 Rebel cavalrymen into Holly Springs. They captured Grant's supplies and destroyed what they could not haul away. Grant's other supply base at Jackson, Tennessee, was destroyed by Rebel cavalryman Nathan Bedford Forrest, who also ripped up 60 miles of railroad which General Grant needed to feed his army of 40,000. Cut off from his supply lines in Mississippi, Grant retreated to Grand Junction, where he had begun.

Major General Grant regrouped and called upon Major General William Tecumseh Sherman to begin the Federal land assault against Vicksburg. On Christmas Day, 1862, the 42-year-old Ohio general landed troops north of town at Milliken's Bend and Young's Point on the west bank of the Mississippi—Vicksburg was on the east bank. Sherman put 30,000 men on the east side of the river on the 26th. With General Sherman on Vicksburg's northern frontier, General Pemberton issued an official recommendation on December 27 that "all the noncombatants, especially the women and children, should forthwith leave the city." Some left; most stayed.

Also on the 27th, Sherman's Federals attacked Chickasaw Bayou in Mississippi. Heavy fighting continued for three bloody days. Confederate defenders repulsed Sherman's landing on December 29. The Yankees lost 208 men killed, 1,005 wounded, and 563

Confederate General Nathan Bedford Forrest, who led the destruction of Grant's supply base at Jackson, Tennessee.

missing. The Confederate defenders on the high ground lost only 63 killed, 134 wounded, and 10 missing.

One month after Sherman's disaster, General Grant arrived on January 29, 1863, at the Federal base north of Vicksburg, on the opposite side of the river at Milliken's Bend. Grant now had 60,000 men, but getting them over to Vicksburg's side of the Mississippi River would take another three and a half months.

Just as the first wisp of spring arrived upriver in February 1863, disease descended upon the city and the nearby Federal camp. Diphtheria swept Vicksburg and across the Mississippi, malaria, measles, and smallpox ravaged Grant's Yankees. After first losing his supply depots and then sitting for three months in mosquito-ridden swamps, General Grant faced growing opposition among the North's impatient politicians. Many urged President Lincoln to replace Grant. "I cannot spare the man," the weary president sighed in March. "He fights."

By April 1863, Grant was ready to fight again. On the 17th, he sent Colonel Benjamin Grierson of Youngstown, Ohio, and his 6th Illinois Cavalry on a daring, hard-riding raid deep into Mississippi. Grant hoped that Grierson's plunge into the state's heartland would force General Pemberton to detach some of his Vicksburg divisions to pursue Grierson. The Yankee cavalry with 1,700 riders dragging six horse-drawn cannons left LaGrange, Tennessee, and rode hard into Mississippi three days later. Twenty thousand Confederates chased Grierson or waited in ambush throughout the state. Although Rebels nipped at the Federals' heels, they never caught them. Colonel Grierson rode 600 miles in 16 days, ripped up 60 miles of Confederate railroad tracks, captured 500 pursuing Rebels, and seized 3,000 weapons. On June 3, Grant rewarded the former music teacher with a promotion to brigadier general. While Grierson's cavalry was busy disrupting Confederate communications and supplies, General Grant had begun his massive assault against Vicksburg.

On the moonless night of April 16, 1863, Grant moved his naval fleet to a base only four miles north of Vicksburg. Thirty ships stoked their steam boilers and slowly made their way down the Mississippi River, past Vicksburg's looming cannons on the high bluffs. Federal Admiral David Porter first sent eight gunboats and three troop transports past the town. Coal barges were lashed to the sides of the troop ships for protection against Vicksburg's cannons. On the

Admiral David D. Porter led the Union naval attack on Vicksburg.

first night of the action, Vicksburg's big guns fired 525 shells at Porter's fleet within 90 minutes. But the ships reached New Carthage, Mississippi, on the west bank of the river, opposite and south of Vicksburg. For 10 days, the Yankee fleet sailed past the city, giving fire and taking fire as they passed.

Finally on April 30, Grant crossed 23,000 Yankees to the east side of the Mississippi—the Vicksburg side. They landed at Bruinsburg, 10 miles south of Vicksburg, and pushed inland to Port Gibson, Mississippi. For the first time, the entire Federal army was on Vicksburg's side of the river, 11 months after Captain Lee from his little gunboat had demanded that the town surrender. After Port Gibson was captured on May 1, with the loss of 787 Confederate defenders killed, wounded, or missing, Grant's Mississippi force swelled to 43,000 men. Separated by the mile-wide river from their line of supply, the Federals foraged off the Confederate landscape.

The Mississippi town of Clinton fell to the Yankees on May 12. Grant pushed northeastward instead of due north toward Vicksburg. He had to move his huge army away from the city in order to approach it later from the east to trap the fortress between the Federals on the east side and the river on the west.

On May 14, Generals Grant and William Tecumseh Sherman captured Jackson, the state capital. From there, Grant turned due west to march along the Vicksburg and Jackson Railroad track which ended inside Vicksburg.

Desperate to defend his city, General Pemberton sent troops east to intercept Grant's force. On May 16,

The battle of Champion Hill was a bloody fight with great loss of life.

the armies met at Baker's Creek, only 20 miles east of Vicksburg. Twenty-three thousand Confederates defended the 70-foot-high Champion Hill beside the creek. Grant attacked at 10:30 in the morning. Fighting was ferocious. At 2:30, the courageous Confederates pushed back the Yankees. But the Federals charged again. Champion Hill was won and lost by the Rebels three times. By 5:00 the exhausted Confederates fell back toward Vicksburg. They left behind 3,840 dead and wounded comrades and 27 Rebel cannons. Grant had lost 2,441 men—but Vicksburg lay dead ahead.

By May 18, General Pemberton had concentrated 31,000 men at Vicksburg while Grant's 43,000 crossed Big Black River on three makeshift pontoon bridges only 12 miles east of the city. Within 24 hours, the Yankees were digging trenches on the outskirts of Vicksburg. In some places, Rebel and Yankee breastworks of mud and logs were only 500 yards apart.

Twice General Grant battered his weary army against the defenses of Vicksburg, on May 19 and 22, and twice Pemberton beat them back. The second assault cost General Grant another 3,200 dead, wounded, and missing Yankees. Safe behind their earthen barriers, the Confederates lost only 500 men.

When Grant's second attack sputtered to a bloody halt, he began the siege of Vicksburg. For 48 days the Confederates were trapped between Grant and the Mississippi with no relief coming from the eastern Confederacy.

On May 25, both sides agreed to a two-and-a-half-hour truce so stretcherbearers from both armies could pick up their dead and wounded comrades who had lain in the miserable, bloody mud for two full days without water or help. Men and boys wearing blue and gray stood up in their trenches, walked between

Union General Grant and Confederate General Pemberton discuss the terms of the surrender of Vicksburg, Mississippi, after the long siege.

the breastworks, and visited with each other. By the hundreds, mud-caked Yankees traded precious coffee for Rebel tobacco. When the truce ended, they waved good-bye and tried for the next six weeks to kill each other.

The Federal noose cutting off Vicksburg's line of supplies and troops from the east was 12 miles long. One end hugged the Mississippi only one and a half miles north of town, and the far end reached the river three miles south of town. Throughout May and June 1863, more Federals poured into Grant's line which grew to 77,000 men and 220 cannons by late June. The Confederate holdouts were all that remained of the once huge Vicksburg defenses, which had stretched from Snyder's Bluff on the Yazoo River, 10 miles north of the city, all the way down the Mississippi to Port Hudson near Baton Rouge, Louisiana, 250 river-miles away.

The Yankee line of trenches and cannons sent Vicksburg's defenders and citizens into their caves carved into front yards and in the middle of dirt roads. No food could squeeze through the Federal siege. By

May 25, Vicksburg's people were eating army mules. They made pretend bread out of crushed peas instead of flour. The few grocery stores with food on their shelves charged outrageous prices. As starvation gripped the city, angry civilians rioted on June 1 and burned down an entire city block.

Inside the city, disease crippled General Pemberton's hungry soldiers. By late June, nearly 6,000 men were in makeshift hospitals with malaria, measles, or dysentery.

General Grant worked to force the city to its knees. On June 20, his 220 cannons bombarded the town for six hours beginning at 4:00 in the morning. Shelling continued for two more weeks. Inside the city and outside, troops from 28 states in the North and South suffered Vicksburg's death struggle.

At 5:00 on the third day of July 1863, General Pemberton's cannons on the high cliffs fired for the last time—Vicksburg surrendered.

The fall of Vicksburg cut the Confederate States of America in half. The Federal navy controlled the mighty Mississippi from Illinois to New Orleans. On August 26, 1863, Abraham Lincoln sent a letter to James C. Conkling, a lawyer and Lincoln family friend back in Springfield, Illinois. The president wrote: "The Father of Waters again goes unvexed to the sea."

Union Major General John C. Frémont

IV

"Give Them Thunder"

Throughout the four years of Civil War, at least 29 battles large and small bloodied Missouri soil. Admitted as a slave state by the Compromise of 1820, Missouri was one of the four slave states which Abraham Lincoln labored to keep loyal to the United States during the war. Along with Delaware, Maryland, and Kentucky, Missouri did remain a Union state, but her citizens fought on both sides.

Mr. Lincoln's troubles with holding onto Missouri began almost immediately. When the war began and Lincoln called up 75,000 volunteers to suppress the rebellion of Southern states, Governer Claibourne Jackson of Missouri refused to allow the Federal government to take Missouri men. The governor was so afraid that Yankee armies would invade his state that he asked the Confederacy to send in forces to protect Missouri from Washington.

The Union general with authority over Missouri in 1861 was Georgia-born General John "Pathfinder" Frémont with headquarters at St. Louis. General

Frémont was married to the daughter of Missouri's U.S. senator, Thomas Hart Benton.

During the first three weeks of war, pro-slavery, anti-Union militiamen in Missouri set up camp near St. Louis. They called their post Camp Jackson in honor of their governor. On May 10, 1861, Federal troops under the command of Captain Nathaniel Lyon captured all 1,000 militiamen. Among the civilians in a crowd of curious spectators was William Tecumseh Sherman, then president of the St. Louis street railroad company. Also watching was Ulysses Grant who was there recruiting volunteers for the Illinois militia.

After the Yankees captured Camp Jackson, Governor Jackson appointed Sterling Price as major general in the Missouri State Guard to lead the fight against a Federal invasion of Missouri. Born in Virginia, General Price had fought in the Mexican War and was Missouri's governor from 1852 to 1856. At age 52, his young soldiers called him Old Pap.

General Lyon, with some 6,000 men in his command, was anxious to hold Missouri for the Union and to do battle against General Price. While General Lyon prepared to march against Missouri Confederates, Governor Jackson called for 50,000 volunteers to man General Price's militia. On June 15, 1861, General Lyon marched two infantry regiments from St. Louis to the Missouri capital, Jefferson City. Governor Jackson locked the governor's office and fled with the entire state legislature to Boonville, Missouri. He took a force of loyal militia troops with

General Sterling Price was Missouri's governor before the war. He fought on the side of the Confederates in Missouri and instructed his troops in battle to "Give them thunder!"

him. On the 17th, Lyon's Yankees marched into Boonville and captured the town after a 20-minute skirmish. The governor and his government managed to escape.

General Lyon's 2,350 infantrymen marched south on July 3 to intercept Governor Jackson before he could cross into Confederate Arkansas. The next day, Yankee Colonel Franz Sigel's regiment of 1,100 German immigrants from St. Louis camped near Carthage, 10 miles south of Governor Jackson's renegade troops. Colonel Sigel pursued Governor Jackson and caught his troops along Coon Creek. After a fight with infantry and artillery, Colonel Sigel pushed Jackson's force through Carthage. On the 5th, Sigel marched 18 miles to Mount Vernon with a loss of 13 men killed and 31 wounded. On July 7, Lyon's tiny army met up with Union army regulars along the Grand River, a stream feeding the Osage River. The regulars were from Fort Leavenworth, Kansas.

Captain Nathaniel Lyon fought to keep Missouri for the Union.

General Lyon and Colonel Sigel concentrated 5,500 Federal troops at Springfield, Missouri. By the end of July 1861, General Price's Missouri State Guard had taken the field to stop General Lyon's force. On August 5, Lyon's army camped at Springfield, Missouri. General Price's force number almost 20,000. As Price approached, General Lyon evacuated Springfield and planned to attack Price's larger force along Wilson's Creek, 12 miles southwest of Springfield. The armies met on August 10, 1861.

General Price's state guard was commanded by Brigadier General Ben McCulloch, a 40-year-old

Major General Franz Sigel led Union troops at the battle of Wilson's Creek as well as throughtout Missouri and other western territories.

native of Tennessee who had ridden with the Texas Rangers before the war.

At 5:00 in the morning on August 10, General Lyon's outnumbered Federals surprised General McCulloch's troops beside Wilson's Creek. Colonel Sigel's men attacked beside Lyon's regulars. McCulloch's troops counterattacked three times but could not break the Yankee assault. General Lyon galloped his warhorse through the battlefield. Lyon waved his hat and shouted to his exhausted men, "Don't aim above their knees!" General Lyon's head was grazed by a bullet but he remained on the field for nearly four hours. General Sterling Price was also on the field rallying his troops. Price shouted "Give them thunder!" Out of that thunder came a

Confederate bullet which plowed into General Lyon's heart and killed him.

Major Sam Sturgis took over command of the Yankees after Lyon died. After seven hours of bloodshed, the two armies pulled back from each other. Each side was too dazed to continue the fight. The Yankees lost 1,317 men killed, wounded, or missing. Price's militiamen lost 1,230. With 23 percent casualties on both sides, the battle of Wilson's Creek, Missouri, had the highest percentage losses of any battle in the Civil War.

Major Sturgis pulled his bleeding survivors out of the Wilson's Creek battlefield and retreated to Springfield. When Price's men pursued the Federals, the Yankees retreated to St. Louis. The withdrawal of the Federals from Springfield gave southwest Missouri to the Confederacy.

General Sigel orders prisoners to haul his cannons at the battle of Wilson's Creek.

General Henry W. Halleck took command of the Union army in the Missouri area in November of 1861.

With Missouri's loyalty to the Union hanging in the balance for three months, in November 1861, President Lincoln gave command of the Missouri area to General Henry Halleck, to replace General Frémont who had failed to stop Sterling Price. General Halleck then dispatched Brigadier General Samuel S. Curtis to southwest Missouri to take on Price.

General Price led 12,000 Confederates across the river from Arkansas. He had hoped to capture St. Louis and then invade Illinois. But his path was blocked by Major General Curtis in front of him and another 7,000 Yankee cavalrymen commanded by Brigadier General Alfred Pleasanton coming in from behind. Instead of retreating south, General Price decided to stand and fight each Federal force in its turn. Price made his stand near Kansas City at Westport on October 23, 1864. Rebels threw themselves at the Federal forces for half the day. Each side lost 1,500 men. When it was over, General Price led a mere 6,000 survivors back into Arkansas, having marched 60 miles in only two days. Missouri remained a Union "border state" through the end of the war.

As Civil War crisscrossed Missouri, at least 19 battles, large and small, also raged in Arkansas. Many of the military leaders bloodied in Missouri also fought in Arkansas, such as Confederates Sterling Price and Ben McCulloch, and Federal Samuel Curtis. Seven months after Wilson's Creek in Missouri, Sterling Price and Ben McCulloch's Confederates camped in the Boston Mountains of northwest Arkansas. Confederate President Jefferson Davis had given over-all command of this area to Major General Earl Van Dorn.

Arriving at the Arkansas front on March 3, 1862, after a 200-mile, 4-day ride, General Van Dorn commanded 17,000 Confederates, which included Ben McCulloch's 8,000 men, Old Pap Price's 7,000, and some 2,000 Native Americans who rode behind Boston-born, Confederate Brigadier General Albert Pike, a lawyer and famous poet.

From their camp in the foothills of the Ozark Mountains, Van Dorn's men marched north on March 4 in pursuit of the Federal army of General Samuel Curtis camped 12 miles away at Cross Hollows, Arkansas. Van Dorn's 17,000 Rebels followed the trail of Curtis's 10,500 Federals. General Curtis had his command strung out across Arkansas with two divisions 12 miles behind his leading two divisions. When Wild Bill Hickock's Yankee scouts spotted Van Dorn in hot pursuit, General Curtis ordered his scattered forces to concentrate along Sugar Creek, close to the Missouri border in the northwest corner of Arkansas.

General Curtis and his Federals arrived at Sugar Creek on March 6, 1862. They pitched camp near the high ground of Pea Ridge, two miles to the north. With the Yankees camped on one side of Sugar

Confederate General Ben McCulloch was a brave leader who lost his life while rallying his troops at the battle of Pea Ridge.

General Samuel Curtis was fooled by the Confederates into thinking they were camped on the opposite side of a creek—instead they attacked him at the rear.

Creek, Van Dorn's Rebels camped on the opposite side. Van Dorn's exhausted men had marched 50 miles in three days. All night, the Federals could clearly see Van Dorn's campfires as snow fell on the cold and hungry armies in blue and gray.

With first light on March 7, General Curtis was stunned to see thousands of smoldering campfires across the creek, but no Confederates. The fires had been a decoy. During the freezing night, Van Dorn had marched his whole army of 17,000 men around Pea Ridge and west of General Curtis in order to attack the Yankees from their rear by surprise.

In the early morning, General Curtis managed to turn four divisions completely around to face Pea Ridge. He had no time to spare. Sterling Price's Confederates charged down Pea Ridge at 10:30 that morning. Fighting swirled around a wilderness saloon called Elkhorn Tavern. The right side of the Yankee line crumbled and was driven backward by the Confederates three times. General Pike's Indians plunged into the battle, killed a company of Yankees, and scalped 40 of the dead Federals.

In the thick of the fight, General McCulloch rallied his weary Rebels. Across the field, Private Peter Pelican of the 36th Illinois Regiment aimed his rifle at the general and fired. General McCulloch hit the ground dead. Private Pelican then stole the dead officer's gold pocketwatch. Confederate Brigadier General James McIntosh, 34, took over McCulloch's command. Minutes after taking command, General McIntosh was also dead. As darkness ended a full day of battle along Pea Ridge, the Federals were pushed back all along their line, but dug-in for the night.

The next morning, the defeated Yankees surprised the victorious Confederates with a counterattack supported by a two-hour barrage from 27 Federal artillery pieces. The cannons were heard 50 miles away. Without General McCulloch to inspire his men, the Rebel line fell back. General Curtis rode among his frenzied Yankees and shouted, "Victory! Victory!" as Van Dorn's Confederates retreated. By late afternoon, both sides agreed to a truce so the burial parties could collect the dead and wounded. The Confederates lost 2,000 men killed or wounded and another 300 captured. The Federals lost 1,384 men, of whom 203 were dead.

The two-day brawl was the largest Civil War battle fought west of the Mississippi River. On March 9, General Van Dorn retreated to Fayetteville, Arkansas. That night, General Curtis wrote a letter home in which he said, "[T]he dead, friends and foes, sleep in the same lonely grave."

The final advance of Union troops at the battle of Pea Ridge, Arkansas.

V

War in the Far West

*T*he American Civil War spilled blood as far west as present-day Arizona. The decisive battles of the Far West were fought in the barren landscape of western Texas and New Mexico.

The Confederate States of America desperately needed to control the West because the federal naval blockade of Southern ports choked the flow of war material coming into the South and the flow of cotton sales to England. The Confederacy needed to secure overland routes to the West's gold and silver mines and to California seaports.

The Far West was important to both President Davis and President Lincoln. The coming of war destroyed the officer corps of the Federal army stationed in the West. The Yankees lost fully one-third of their western officers when 313 men resigned from the army to join the Confederate military. During the war years, Lincoln and the Federal Congress never stopped working to hold the territories of the West in the broken Union. In 1861, Dakota Territory, Colorado Territory, and Nevada Territory were created. In 1863,

Idaho Territory and Arizona Territory were created by Congress. In 1864, Montana Territory was created and Nevada was admitted to the Union as a state so the Union could better mine Nevada silver.

Even while the Lincoln administration was struggling to keep a million men in Union blue for the four-year battle, it also continued to post thousands of troops in the Far West. As noted by Robert Utley, chief historian for the National Park Service in 1984: "The diversion of such military strength to the West when troops were so desperately wanted in the South revealed the measure of Abraham Lincoln's need for western gold and silver and western political support for the prosecution of the war." Not less that 20,000 Federal soldiers served in the Far West throughout the Civil War.

The Union and the Confederacy both also worked to hold the loyalty of the West's Native American nations. The so-called Five Civilized Tribes living in Indian Territory, now Oklahoma, were especially courted by both governments. Of these nations, the slave-owning Choctaws and Chickasaws sided with the Confederacy. The Cherokee, Creek, and Seminole nations split, with some factions Unionists and some Confederates.

Cherokee Indian Stand Watie was loyal to the Confederacy to the last. He became a Confederate brigadier general in 1864. When he finally surrendered two months after Robert E. Lee's April 1865 surrender, Stand Watie was the last Confederate general to give up. Cherokee Chief John Ross tried hard to keep the Cherokee nation loyal to the Union. But he was pushed into the Confederate camp after the Yankees lost Wilson's Creek, Missouri.

War had come quickly to the gold-rich Far West. Only three weeks after Fort Sumter, Confederate Lieutenant Colonel John Baylor led his Texas Mounted Rifles to the Yankee camp at Fort Fillmore, New Mexico Territory (now Arizona). Seven hundred Federals under the command of Major Isaac Lynde held the fort near Mesilla, 40 miles north of El Paso. On July 24, 1861, Baylor's 350 troopers pitched camp only 600 yards from the fort. Baylor was on one bank of the Rio Grande River and the fort was on the opposite side.

Colonel Baylor attacked the next morning and was beaten back. Four of his men were killed. Major Lynde escaped from the fort and led his men northeast toward Fort Stanton, 150 miles away. Baylor pursued the Federals, caught them at San Augustin Springs, and Major Lynde surrendered 492 survivors.

On August 1, 1861, Colonel Baylor created the new Confederate state of Arizona out of the New Mexico Territory by drawing a line running east and west on the map at the 34-degree latitude. The Confederate Congress quickly admitted the new state into the Confederacy.

Colonel Baylor was already well-known to Richmond. He had stunned and embarrassed the Confederate government when he began rounding up Apaches throughout New Mexico to force them to the Rebel side. His written orders to his men in 1861 were clear and simple: "You will use all means to persuade the Apaches or any tribe to come in for the purpose of making peace and when you get them together, kill all the grown Indians and take the children prisoners and sell them to defray the expense of killing the Indians."

In July 1861, perhaps to prevent an Indian massacre by Colonel Baylor, President Jefferson Davis appointed Henry Hopkins Sibley to the command of a new

Union Colonel Edward Canby commanded Fort Craig in 1862.

Confederate Army of New Mexico to hold the country for the South. Sibley had been a major in the Yankee army when war came but he resigned his commission and went South. The 44-year-old brigadier general was sent to the West without so much as a rifle. His orders were to raise his own army.

General Sibley raised three new regiments on his own, the 4th Regiment under the command of James Reiley, the 5th under Colonel Thomas Green, and the 7th under Colonel William Steele. He also brought Lieutenant Colonel Baylor's Texas Mounted Rifles into his new command which now numbered about 3,700 men.

Yankee forts scattered throughout western Texas and New Mexico began shifting men out of Sibley's way. The Federals at Fort Stanton slipped north to Albuquerque, New Mexico Territory. The Yankees at Fort Thorn, 50 miles north of Mesilla, Arizona, escaped 80 miles north to Fort Craig on the Rio Grande River. The garrison at Fort Craig counted 4,000 Federals.

By February 1862, General Sibley's small new army was marching northward, up the Rio Grande River. On February 19, his force camped on the east bank of the river, opposite Fort Craig. Colonel Edward Canby commanded the Yankee fort.

Sibley and Canby knew each other well—General Sibley was Colonel Canby's brother-in-law, and Sibley had been a Yankee major in Colonel Canby's pre-war command.

Colonel Canby braced for Sibley's attack. Among Canby's scouts inside Fort Craig was the legendary

Kit Carson. But the colonel had taught his brother-in-law well about desert warfare. Sibley did not attack; he ignored Fort Craig and left them to starve to death when he pulled back and continued his northward march.

Canby knew that he could not remain in the fort indefinitely. So he decided to attack. He sent one regiment five miles up the Rio Grande with orders to cross the river ahead of Sibley's Rebels, and to attack the Confederates on the east bank. The Yankees would be outnumbered four to one.

On February 20, Canby's brave riders crossed the river and attacked General Sibley. The Confederates easily pushed the Yankees back, but the troops in blue held on. They were able to pin down the Confederates for another day to give Colonel Canby time to ride up with his whole command of 4,000 men and horse-drawn cannons.

General Henry Hopkins Sibley commanded the Army of New Mexico for the South, but failed to hold the territory for the Confederacy.

When Canby's command arrived on February 21, the odds were now better than even at what became known as the battle of Valverde, New Mexico. The Federals attacked, but were driven back again by Sibley's regiments. Rebel Colonel Tom Green pushed the Yankees back into the Rio Grande River and turned the Federals' own cannons around to fire at the survivors swimming across.

After the slaughter beside the river, a truce was called for the stretcherbearers and burial details. The

The legendary Kit Carson was a scout for Union Colonel Edward Canby.

Federals had lost 263 men to Sibley's 187 casualties. Gathering their dead and wounded, Canby's bloodied command limped south, back to Fort Craig.

General Sibley remained beside the river for two more days. On February 23, he resumed his trek upriver. He reached Albuquerque on March 1. The Confederates had counted on finding massive Yankee supply depots full of food and fresh water. But they found only smoking ruins. Retreating Federals had burned what they could not carry when they had evacuated the town. Sibley had no choice but to continue marching north. He reached Santa Fe on March 5—again hoping to find Yankee supplies and again finding ashes. The retreating Yankees were concentrating now at Fort Union, 60 miles east of Santa Fe.

General Sibley, short on food and water, had to block a Federal attack from the east. So he sent 600 men 20 miles to the southeast to hold Apache Canyon. This would cut off any Federal advance from Fort Union. On March 26, Sibley's advance force in the canyon spotted 400 Yankees marching west, toward Santa Fe and Sibley's camp. General Sibley ordered his forward troops in the canyon to attack the Federals. Major Charles Pyron led Sibley's men four miles into Apache Canyon and a trap.

More than 1,300 Yankees, calling themselves the 1st Colorado Volunteers, rimmed the canyon walls and opened fire on the Rebels below. The Colorado men

were led by Major John Chivington. It was a slaughter. The Federals lost 19 men and the retreating Confederates lost 146.

General Sibley sent two more regiments toward Apache Canyon on the 27th and on March 28, Sibley's force slammed into westbound Federals at Glorieta Pass. Colonel William Scurry led Sibley's assault. The fighting raged for five hours and the Confederates were pushing the Yankees back. But at the last minute, Major Chivington's volunteers captured General Sibley's 85 wagons of supplies at Johnson's Ranch near Apache Canyon, behind General Sibley's lines. Now without supplies, the Rebels had to abandon their victory and retreat back to Santa Fe. At Glorieta Pass, Sibley lost 123 men and the Federals lost 86.

With Yankees in pursuit, General Sibley tried to escape down the Rio Grande. But by the middle of April, Sibley had no choice but to abandon the river and head west, out into the desert. With only five days worth of water, his army marched for 10 days through

Fort Union was used by the retreating Yankee army in March of 1862.

51

a wasteland covering 100 deadly miles. Nearly 1,200 Confederates dropped in scorching heat and never got up. The survivors had made one of the great, desperate marches in the history of warfare.

In early May, General Sibley's force staggered into Fort Bliss, Texas. Since leaving Texas in February, Sibley had lost 1,700 men. On May 14, 1862, General Sibley led some 2,000 weary survivors toward San Antonio, Texas, where he disbanded his entire army.

With General Sibley's New Mexico failure, the Confederacy lost forever its hold on the Far West, as well as its hope for the West's gold and the ports of California.

VI

Indian Uprisings

*T*hroughout the Civil War, rising tensions and bloody conflicts with Native Americans occupied Abraham Lincoln's weary mind. While it might be argued that Indian rage over their treatment by the Federal government was not actually part of the Civil War, three historical conclusions cannot be disputed: The Lincoln Administration did try to keep native people loyal to the Union cause, especially the Five Civilized Tribes; Indian threats to peace in the West were also threats to the Union's lines of communication with western outposts, political support, and resources, especially gold and silver; and, most important, every Yankee dispatched to calm the Native American conflicts was one less Federal who could be ordered East to fight Confederates along the Mississippi River, or to fight Robert E. Lee beside Antietam Creek or on the hillside at Gettysburg.

In the Indian reservation system of the 1800s, Native Americans displaced from their ancestral lands were promised Federal "annuities" in exchange for living on vast reservations. These annuities were govern-

ment payments to the Indian nations which they would then use to purchase food, clothing, and supplies from government-licensed Indian agents. Corruption in this system by the agents was a century-long, national disgrace. By the time the Indian agents deducted rents and credits from these annuities, there was often nothing left for the Indians. The corruption by the whites and hunger of the Sioux Nation exploded in Minnesota in July 1862.

Minnesota Indian agents refused to release government food rations to the Santee Sioux at Yellow Medicine Indian Agency. On August 4, a handful of young Sioux raided the agency's food warehouse. Government agents begged local merchants to release food supplies before the year's Indian annuities arrived from Civil War-pressed Washington. White trader Andrew Wyrick responded, "If they are hungry, let them eat grass."

On August 17, four Sioux, probably teenagers, killed five white settlers at Acton, Minnesota. Although angry with his young men for such a foolish and risky adventure, a Sioux leader called Little Crow agreed to lead angry Sioux in an uprising. On the 18th, Little Crow's followers attacked Andrew Wyrick's store at the Redwood Agency and killed him. Then they stuffed grass in the dead man's mouth. In the Sioux rampage that followed, nearly 400 whites were killed.

On August 20, Little Crow and 100 warriors attacked New Ulm, Minnesota. The settlers drove the Sioux off. The next day, Little Crow and 400 men attacked Fort Ridgely. Little Crow was again driven back with the loss of 100 Sioux. He tried again the next day with 800 warriors and was pushed back. On August 23, Little Crow and 400 men attacked New Ulm for the second time. Although Little Crow was defeated again, he killed 36 whites and wounded 23. The impact of the

New Ulm attack on the Civil War was immediate.

Earlier, in July 1862, President Lincoln had sent his private secretary, John Nicolay, out to Minnesota to personally inspect the Sioux situation. After the Redwood Agency massacre and the New Ulm attacks, Nicolay sent an urgent telegram to President Lincoln: "The massacre of innocent white settlers has been fearful. A wild panic prevails in nearly one-half of the state."

Lincoln felt pressure directly from Minnesota's governor which would impact the Union's Civil War efforts. Governor Alexander Ramsey telegraphed President Lincoln and asked the president to delay recruiting and drafting Minnesota men into the Union armies. On August 27, Lincoln wired his answer to the governor: "Attend to the Indians. If the draft cannot proceed, of course it will not proceed."

Governor Ramsey charged the Minnesota militia with putting down the Sioux uprising. In command was Colonel Henry Hastings Sibley. (This is not the Henry Hopkins Sibley from the New Mexico battlefields.) The Minnesota Henry H. Sibley had already served Minnesota as postmaster, fur trader, congressman, and governor.

On August 31, 1862, Colonel Sibley sent 150 men under Captain Hiram Grant's command to the Redwood Agency. They buried 80 dead settlers. Two days later, the Sioux attacked Captain Grant's camp, killing 22 soldiers and wounding 60. Grant's troops

Colonel Henry Hastings Sibley commanded Union troops fighting the Sioux tribe in Minnesota. He convened a military trial that condemned 303 Sioux warriors to death in 1862.

Captain Hiram Grant fought under Colonel Hastings against the Sioux and was one of five officers who sentenced the Sioux warriors to be hung.

fought Sioux for 31 continuous hours until Colonel Sibley arrived with more troops on September 3.

On September 23, Colonel Sibley attacked the Santee Sioux at Wood Lake, Minnesota. Twenty Sioux were killed and 2,000 were captured, but Little Crow escaped. The militiamen lost 7 killed and 30 wounded. One of the grimmest spectacles in the history of North American law and justice would follow Sibley's victory at Wood Lake.

As his reward for Wood Lake, Colonel Sibley was promoted to brigadier general on September 29. General Sibley then convened a military court to try the 2,000 Sioux prisoners for the month of bloodshed. On November 3, the military court composed of five officers, including Captain Grant, sentenced 303 Sioux to hang.

A flurry of telegrams flowed between St. Paul, Minnesota, and the White House. Abraham Lincoln had to deal with the prospect of a mass execution the likes of which had never been seen in North America. On November 10, Lincoln wired that he wanted to review "the full and complete record of these convictions." Minnesota Governor Ramsey telegraphed the president: "I hope the execution of every Sioux Indian condemned by the military court will be at once ordered."

President Lincoln must have paced the White House halls as he dealt with the Minnesota executions. On December 1, he sent a letter to Joseph Holt, judge advocate of the United States Army, and asked, "I wish your legal opinion whether, if I should conclude to execute only a part of them, I must myself designate which, or could I leave the designation to some officer on the ground?"

On December 6, Lincoln reduced the number of condemned Sioux from 303 to 39. The day after Christmas 1862, 38 of the 39 Sioux were hanged together at 10:00 in the morning at Mankato, Minnesota, 90 miles from St. Paul. It was the largest mass execution in American history.

One month after the mass hanging in Minnesota, Shoshoni Indians conducted raids on white outposts in Idaho. Chief Bear Hunter led the raids. Again, Federal troops unavailable for fighting Confederates were sent in pursuit of the Shoshoni. Colonel Patrick Connor was sent from Fort Douglas, Utah, to follow Bear Hunter to his Idaho camp beside Battle Creek near the Bear River and what is today Preston, Idaho. Colonel Connor attacked 300 Shoshone warriors and their women and children. The troops suffered 67 casualties but killed or wounded 384 Shoshones. The

The execution of 38 Sioux Indians at Mankato, Minnesota, December 26, 1862.

War with the Sioux tribe continued throughout the Civil War and after, with many attacks like this one on Sioux villages.

January 29, 1863, attack is known as the Bear River Massacre.

Throughout the Civil War, Union-Indian battles large and small swept across Oklahoma, North Dakota, Minnesota, and Idaho. Each kept Federal troops from going East to fight Confederates. The worst massacre of Native Americans occurred in November 1864 in Colorado.

In 1862, Colorado Territory Governor John Evans ordered Colonel John Chivington to remove Cheyenne and Arapahos from areas rich in minerals. Colonel Chivington, born in Lebanon, Ohio, raised the 3rd Colorado Cavalry. The same John Chivington had helped to defeat the New Mexico Henry Sibley in Apache Canyon.

To avoid war, Cheyenne Chief Black Kettle agreed to enter peace talks with the whites at Fort Lyon, Colorado. Governor Evans was disappointed. He said of Chivington's 3rd Cavalry, "They have been raised to kill Indians and they must kill Indians."

During the peace talks, Black Kettle's Cheyenne village was camped along Sand Creek, 40 miles northeast of Fort Lyon. Colonel Chivington led 700 troopers toward Black Kettle's camp. On November 29, 1864, Colonel Chivington's 700 cavalrymen reached the Sand Creek camp of Black Kettle. Seeing the soldiers coming, Black Kettle hung both a United States flag and a white flag on his lodge. Chivington attacked anyway. When three white cavalrymen protested the murder of Cheyenne women and children, Chivington shouted, "Damn any man who sympathizes with Indians. I have come to kill Indians!"—and he did.

The 3rd Colorado Cavalry charged 115 Cheyenne lodges beside Sand Creek. Two hundred Cheyenne were killed. As many as 140 of the dead were women and children. The cavalry then scalped the bodies and mutilated the Cheyenne corpses. Chief Black Kettle escaped the annihilation of his people.

Between Confederate efforts to secure the Far West and the Union's efforts to defeat them and to protect settlers from Indian uprisings, the West played an important part in the American Civil War. Civil War battles occurred as far west as Picacho Peak, Arizona. Even though the East has always had the glory and the truly huge battles of that terrible conflict, the war for the West and the battle for the Mississippi River were vital to the Union victory.

As North Carolina State University Professor Richard M. McMurry wrote, "[A]s the Civil War evolved, the really decisive area—the theater where the outcome of the war was decided—was the West."

Glossary

bluecoats   Term used for soldiers in the Northern Union army during the Civil War because of the color of their uniforms.

Confederacy   The Confederate States of America; the South.

Confederate   Citizen of the Confederate States of America; a Southerner during the Civil War.

Federals   A name used for members of the Union.

graycoats   Term used for soldiers in the Southern Confederate army during the Civil War because of the color of their uniforms.

ironclad   A wooden ship covered with sheets of iron for protection.

malaria   Disease spread by mosquitoes that causes chills and high fever.

Missouri Compromise of 1820   Declaration that slavery would never be allowed north of $36\frac{1}{2}$ degrees north latitude except for the state of Missouri.

mortar   A frontloading cannon with a short tube used to shoot projectiles at high angles.

Rebels   Term used for Southerners in the Civil War.

secessionist   Southerners who voted to secede from the Union and form their own republic.

siege   A military strategy where a city or fort is surrounded by enemy troops, cutting off all supply routes. The object is to get the city or fort to surrender due to starvation and lack of supplies.

Union   The United States of America; the North.

Yankees   Term used for Northerners during the Civil War.

Further Reading

Axelrod, Alan. *Chronicle of the Indian Wars*. New York: Prentice Hall, 1993.

Carter, Samuel. *The Final Fortress: The Campaign for Vicksburg, 1862-1863*. New York: St. Martin's Press, 1980.

Christ, Mark K., ed. *Rugged and Sublime: The Civil War in Arkansas*. Little Rock: University of Arkansas Press, 1994.

Foote, Shelby. *The Civil War: A Narrative*, Volumes I and II. New York: Random House 1958, 1963.

Hall, Martin H. *The Confederate Army of New Mexico*. Austin, TX: Presidial Press, 1978.

Monaghan, Jay. *Civil War on the Western Border, 1854-1865*. New York: Bonanza Books, 1955.

Thompson, Jerry. *Henry Hopkins Sibley: Confederate General of the West*. Natchitoches, LA: Louisiana Northwestern State University Press, 1987.

Utley, Robert M. *The Indian Frontier of the American West, 1846-1890*. Albuquerque: University of New Mexico Press, 1984.

Websites About the West in the Civil War

The Civil War in Indian Territory:
    http://users.erols.com/jreb/oklahoma.html
    http://geocities.com/Heartland/Hills/1263/civilwarIT.html
The Civil War in Kansas:
    http://www.rahab.net/civilwar.htm
Engagements and Battles in MO during the War of the Rebellion
    1861-1865: http://www.usmo.com/~momollus/
The Tennessee Civil War Home Page:
    http://members.aol.com/jweaver303/tn/tncwhp.htm
The War Between the States in Tennessee:
    http://www.geocities.com/CapitolHill/4117/page3.htm

Index

PHOTO CREDITS
Harper's Weekly: pp. 10, 16, 19, 22, 26, 28, 29, 30, 32, 34, 36, 37, 38, 39, 41, 42, 44, 48, 57, 58; National Archives: pp. 14, 20, 40; United States Army Military History Institute: pp. 49, 50, 51, 55, 56

FRIENDS FREE LIBRARY
GERMANTOWN FRIENDS LIBRARY
5418 Germantown Avenue
Philadelphia, PA 19144
215-951-2355

Each borrower is responsible for all items
checked out on his/her library card, for
fines on materials kept overtime, and
replacing any lost or damaged materials.